99 Effective Meal and Juice Recipes to Help Reduce Menstrual Cramps:

Minimize Symptoms and Pain Using Natural Ingredients

By

Joe Correa CSN

COPYRIGHT

© 2019 Live Stronger Faster Inc.

All rights reserved

Reproduction or translation of any part of this work beyond that permitted by section 107 or 108 of the 1976 United States Copyright Act without the permission of the copyright owner is unlawful.

This publication is designed to provide accurate and authoritative information in regard to the subject matter covered. It is sold with the understanding that neither the author nor the publisher is engaged in rendering medical advice. If medical advice or assistance is needed, consult with a doctor. This book is considered a guide and should not be used in any way detrimental to your health. Consult with a physician before starting this nutritional plan to make sure it's right for you.

ACKNOWLEDGEMENTS

This book is dedicated to my friends and family that have had mild or serious illnesses so that you may find a solution and make the necessary changes in your life.

99 Effective Meal and Juice Recipes to Help Reduce Menstrual Cramps:

Minimize Symptoms and Pain Using Natural Ingredients

By

Joe Correa CSN

CONTENTS

Copyright

Acknowledgements

About The Author

Introduction

Commitment

99 Effective Meal and Juice Recipes to Help Reduce Menstrual Cramps: Minimize Symptoms and Pain Using Natural Ingredients

Additional Titles from This Author

ABOUT THE AUTHOR

After years of Research, I honestly believe in the positive effects that proper nutrition can have over the body and mind. My knowledge and experience has helped me live healthier throughout the years and which I have shared with family and friends. The more you know about eating and drinking healthier, the sooner you will want to change your life and eating habits.

Nutrition is a key part in the process of being healthy and living longer so get started today. The first step is the most important and the most significant.

INTRODUCTION

99 Effective Meal and Juice Recipes to Help Reduce Menstrual Cramps: Minimize Symptoms and Pain Using Natural Ingredients

By Joe Correa CSN

This book will help you learn how to deal with your body and how to reduce these unpleasant symptoms. Menstrual symptoms appear 7-10 days before the beginning of menstruation and usually, pass a few days after the period starts.

These symptoms vary from cycle to cycle and from woman to woman. But one thing is for sure – every woman on the planet has experienced some of these symptoms at least once in their lifetime. It depends on the hormonal balance, but also on other factors such as diet, stress, and lifestyle. This is why it is extremely important to get to know your body better and to follow your menstrual cycle by recording it on a calendar and observe how your body behaves.

Diet against PMS!

To avoid unpleasant symptoms of PMS in the second half of the cycle, be careful with what you eat. Avoid too much sugar, processed food, soft drinks, alcohol, coffee, black tea, and too many fats. Correcting your diet during these 14 days before period will avoid and reduce the unpleasant side effects of PMS and even pain.

In the second half of the menstrual cycle eat more fish and healthy fats, since studies have shown that this can alleviate symptoms of PMS. Women suffering from menstrual pain have a low level of fatty acid in the body. Interestingly, women in Japan rarely suffer from PMS because of a diet rich in fish and healthy fats.

In order to reduce those menstrual cramps, eat foods rich in vitamin B, especially pyridoxine (vitamin B6). It elevates mood, improves sleep and relieves pain in the abdomen.

Overall health will also improve by increasing calcium and magnesium. Some studies show that an increase in calcium and magnesium in the second half of the cycle, can reduce many premenstrual symptoms. Calcium not only improves mood but also prevents allergic reactions, pain, and reduces menstrual bleeding. Magnesium helps to establish mental balance, reduces irritability, stress, and increases the overall resistance of our organism.

This book was created to help women prevent menstrual cramps, empower their body, boost up their immune system, and enjoy their life every single day!

COMMITMENT

In order to improve my condition, I *(your name)*, commit to eating more of these foods on a daily basis and to exercise at least 30 minutes daily:

- Berries (especially blueberries), peaches, cherries, apples, apricots, oranges, lemon juice, grapefruit, tangerines, mandarins, pears, etc.
- Broccoli, spinach, collard greens, sweet potatoes, avocado, artichoke, baby corn, carrots, celery, cauliflower, onions, etc.
- Whole grains, steel-cut oats, oatmeal, quinoa, barley, etc.
- Black beans, red bean beans, garbanzo beans, lentils, etc.
- Nuts and seeds including: walnuts, cashews, flaxseeds, sesame seeds, etc.
- Fish
- 8 – 10 glasses of water

Sign here

X_____

99 EFFECTIVE MEAL AND JUICE RECIPES TO HELP REDUCE MENSTRUAL CRAMPS: MINIMIZE SYMPTOMS AND PAIN USING NATURAL INGREDIENTS

MEALS

Breakfast Recipes

1. Walnutty Oatmeal with Greek Yogurt and Apricots

Ingredients:

2oz rolled oats

10oz Greek yogurt

1 tbsp of honey

7oz fresh apricots, chopped

1 tbsp of walnuts, grated

Preparation:

Bring one cup of water to a boiling point. Place the oats in it and cook for 3-4 minutes.

Reduce the heat and stir in walnuts. Simmer until the oats are soft.

Remove from the heat and cool for a while. Add honey and mix well. Top with apricots and serve.

Nutrition information per serving: Kcal: 267, Protein: 24g, Carbs: 39g, Fats: 7g

2. Warm Quinoa with Bananas and Chia Seeds

Ingredients:

2 tsp of chia seeds, soaked

½ cup of almond milk

1.5oz quinoa

½ cup of water

1 small banana, peeled and sliced

2 tbsp of blueberries

1 tbsp of honey

1 tbsp of almonds, roughly chopped

Preparation:

Combine the water and almond milk in a medium sized saucepan. Bring it to a boil and add quinoa. Reduce the heat and cook for about 20 minutes, or until all the water evaporates.

Meanwhile, mash ½ banana with a fork. Leave the other sliced. Roughly chop the almond. Set aside.

Transfer the cooked quinoa to a bowl. Stir in the mashed banana, blueberries, honey, and chia seeds.

Top with sliced banana and chopped almonds.

Nutrition information per serving: Kcal: 306 Protein: 17g, Carbs: 33, Fats: 14g

3. Flaxseed Pancakes with Blueberries and Greek Yogurt

Ingredients:

4 eggs, Omega-3 enriched

4 tbsp buckwheat flour

4 tbsp flax seeds, minced

1 cup of almond milk

¼ tsp of salt

1 cup of Greek yogurt

1 cup of fresh blueberries

Flaxseed oil

Preparation:

Combine the ingredients in a bowl. Beat well with an electric mixer, on high.
Heat up the oil in a medium-sized skillet, over a high temperature. Pour some of the mixture in the skillet and fry the pancakes for about 2-3 minutes, on each side.
This mixture should give you about 8 pancakes.
Top each pancake with Greek yogurt and fresh blueberries. Serve.

Nutrition information per serving: Kcal: 161 Protein: 16.5g, Carbs: 10, Fats: 5g

4. Eggs Stuffed with Shrimps, Avocado, and Cress

Ingredients:

2 eggs

4 small shrimps

1 tbsp of Dijon mustard

¼ tsp of freshly ground black pepper

1 medium-sized avocado, halved

A handful of finely chopped cress

Extra virgin olive oil

¼ cup of fresh lemon juice

Fresh lettuce

Preparation:

Heat up two tablespoons of oil over a medium heat. Add shrimps and stir-fry for about five minutes. Remove from the heat and set aside.

Meanwhile, boil the eggs. Gently place two eggs in a pot of boiling water. Cook for 10 minutes. Rinse and drain. Cool for a while and peel. You can add one teaspoon of baking soda in a boiling water. This will make the peeling process much easier.

Cut the eggs in half and remove the yolks.

In a medium-sized bowl, combine the egg yolks with ½ avocado, mustard, black pepper, and lemon juice. Transfer to a blender and pulse to combine. Use this mixture to stuff each egg half.

Top each egg with finely chopped cress and one shrimp. You can add some salt to taste.

Serve with fresh lettuce and chopped avocado.

Nutrition information per serving: Kcal: 170 Protein: 29g, Carbs: 8, Fats: 11g

5. Greek Yogurt with Muesli, Honey, and Kiwi

Ingredients:

3.5oz Greek yogurt

1 tbsp of honey

¼ cup of muesli (I use rolled oats with dried fruits, but any other combination you have on hand will work)

½ large banana or 1 small banana, peeled and sliced

2 tbsp of raisins

2 tbsp of walnuts, finely chopped

Preparation:

Combine the Greek yogurt with honey and mix well with a spoon. Add muesli, sliced banana and top with raisins and finely chopped walnuts.

Serve immediately.

Nutrition information per serving: Kcal: 121 Protein: 19g, Carbs: 16.7g, Fats: 4.5g

Soup Recipes

6.   **Mushroom and Ginger Soup**

Ingredients:

1 oz dried Chinese mushrooms or 4½ oz field or chestnut mushrooms

1½ pints hot vegetable stock

4½ oz thread egg noodles

2 tsp sunflower oil

3 garlic cloves, crushed

1-inch piece root ginger, finely shredded

2 tbsp sour cream

1 tsp light tomato sauce

4½ oz bean sprouts

Fresh coriander leaves, to garnish

Preparation:

Soak the dried Chinese mushrooms (if using) for at least 30

minutes in 10 fl oz of hot vegetable stock. Remove all the mushroom stalks and discard, then slice the mushrooms. Reserve the stock.

Cook the noodles for 2-3 minutes in boiling water. Drain and rinse. Set them aside.

Heat the oil over a high heat in a wok or large, heavy frying pan. Add the garlic and ginger, stir and add the mushrooms. Stir over a high heat for 2 minutes.

Add the remaining vegetable stock with the reserved stock and bring to a boil. Add the sour cream and tomato sauce.

Stir in the bean sprouts and cook until tender. Put some noodles in each bowl and ladle the soup on top. Garnish with coriander leaves and serve immediately.

Nutrition information per serving: Kcal: 74 Protein: 3g, Carbs: 9g, Fats: 3g

7. Brown Lentil & Pasta Soup

Ingredients:

2 pieces of lean chicken breast, cut into small squares

1 onion, chopped

2 garlic cloves, crushed

2 celery sticks, chopped

1¾ oz farfalline or spaghetti, broken into small pieces

14 oz brown lentils, soaked

2 pints hot ham or vegetable stock

2 tbsp chopped fresh mint

Preparation:

Place the meat in a large, dry frying pan together with the onions, garlic, and celery. Cook for 4-5 minutes, stirring until the onion is tender and the meat is just beginning to brown.

Add the pasta to the frying pan and cook, stirring, for about 1 minute.

Add the brown lentils and stock and bring the mixture to a boil. Lower the heat and leave to simmer for about 12-15 minutes or until the pasta is tender.

Remove the frying pan from the heat and stir in the chopped fresh mint.

Transfer the soup to warm soup bowls and serve immediately.

Tip:

If you prefer to use dried lentils, add the stock before the pasta and cook for 1-1¼ hours until the lentils are tender. Add the pasta and cook for another 12-15 minutes.

Nutrition information per serving: Kcal: 225 Protein: 13g, Carbs: 27g, Fats: 8g

8. Spicy Dhal and Carrot Soup

Ingredients:

4 oz split red lentils

12 oz carrots, peeled and sliced

2 onions, peeled and chopped

9 oz chopped tomatoes

2 garlic cloves, peeled and chopped

2 tbsp vegetable ghee or oil

2 pints vegetable stock

1 tsp ground cumin

1 tsp ground coriander

1 fresh green chili, deseeded and chopped, or 1 tsp ground chili

½ tsp ground turmeric

1 tbsp lemon juice

Salt

10 fl oz skimmed milk

2 tbsp chopped fresh coriander

Natural yogurt, to serve

Preparation:

Place the lentils in a sieve and rinse well under cold running water. Drain them thoroughly and place in a large pan with 1½ pints of the vegetable stock, and the carrots, onions, tomatoes and garlic. Bring the mixture to a boil. Lower the heat, cover, and simmer for 30 minutes.

Meanwhile, heat the ghee or oil in a small pan, add the cumin, coriander, chilli and turmeric and cook gently for 1 minute.

Remove from the heat and stir in the lemon juice and salt to taste.

Puree the soup in batches in a blender or food processor. Return the soup to the pan, add the spice mixture and the remaining 6floz stock or water and simmer for 10 minutes.

Add the milk to the soup and adjust the seasoning according to taste.

Stir in the chopped coriander and reheat gently. Serve hot with a dollop of yogurt.

Nutrition information per serving: Kcal: 173 Protein: 9g, Carbs: 24g, Fats: 5g

9.   Dhal Soup

Ingredients:

2 tbsp vegetable oil

2 garlic cloves, crushed

1 onion, chopped

½ tsp turmeric

1 tsp garam masala

¼ tsp chili powder

1 tsp ground cumin

2 lb 4 oz chopped tomatoes

7 oz red lentils

2 tsp lemon juice

1 pint vegetable stock

10 fl oz coconut milk

Salt and pepper

Naan bread, to serve

To garnish:

Fresh coriander, finely chopped

Lemon slices

Preparation:

Heat up the oil in a large saucepan. Add the garlic and onion and saute, stirring, for 2-3 minutes. Add the turmeric, garam masala, chili powder and cumin and cook for another 30 seconds.

Add tomatoes and stir to the pan with the red lentils, lemon juice, vegetable stock and coconut stock and bring to a boil.

Reduce the heat to low and simmer the soup, uncovered for about 25-30 minutes until the lentils are tender and cooked.

Season to taste with salt and pepper and ladle the soup into warm serving bowls. Garnish with chopped coriander and lemon slices and serve immediately with warm naan bread.

Nutrition information per serving: Kcal: 284 Protein: 16g, Carbs: 38g, Fats: 9g

10. Chicken Wonton Soup

Ingredients:

12oz minced chicken

1 tbsp tomato sauce

1 tsp grated fresh root ginger

1 garlic clove, finely chopped

2 tsp sherry

2 spring onions, chopped

1 tsp sesame oil

1 egg white

½ tsp corn flour

½ tsp sugar

Around 35 wonton skins

2½ pints chicken stock

1 spring onion, shredded

1 small carrot, cut into very thin slices

Preparation:

Put the chicken, tomato sauce, ginger, garlic, sherry, spring onions, sesame oil, egg white, cornflour and sugar in a bowl and mix well.

Place a small spoon full of the filling in the center of each wonton skin.

Dampen the edges. Gather up each one to form a pouch to enclose the filling.

Cook the wontons in boiling water for 1 minute or until they float to the surface. Remove with a slotted spoon.

Pour the chicken stock into a saucepan and bring to a boil.

Add the spring onion, carrot and wontons to the soup. Simmer gently for 2 minutes, then serve.

Tip:

Look for wonton skins in Asian stores. Fresh skins can be found in the chilled compartment and they can be frozen if you wish. Wrap in cling film before freezing.

Nutrition information per serving: Kcal: 101 Protein: 14g, Carbs: 3g, Fats: 4g

Lunch Recipes

11.   Beef, Tomato and Olive Kebabs

Ingredients:

1 lb rump or sirloin steak

16 cherry tomatoes

16 large green olives, stoned

Salt and freshly ground black pepper

Focaccia bread, to serve

<u>Baste:</u>

4 tbsp olive oil

1 tbsp sherry vinegar

1 garlic clove, crushed

<u>Fresh tomato relish:</u>

1 tbsp olive oil

1 tbsp sherry vinegar

1 garlic clove, crushed

6 plum tomatoes, skinned, deseeded and chopped

2 green olives, stoned and sliced

1 tbsp chopped fresh parsley

1 tbsp lemon juice

Preparation:

Trim any fat from the meat and cut into about 24 even-sized pieces.

Thread the meat onto 8 skewers, alternating it with cherry tomatoes and the stoned whole olives.

To make the baste, in a bowl combine the oil, vinegar, garlic, and salt and pepper to taste.

To make the fresh tomato relish, heat the oil in a small saucepan and cook the onion and garlic for 3-4 minutes until softened. Add the tomatoes and sliced olives and cook for 2-3 minutes until the tomatoes are softened slightly. Stir in the parsley and lemon juice, and season with salt and pepper to taste. Set aside and keep warm or leave to chill.

Barbecue the skewers on an oiled rack over hot coals for 5-10 minutes, basting and turning frequently. Serve with the tomato relish and slices of focaccia.

Nutrition information per serving: Kcal: 166 Protein: 12g, Carbs: 1g, Fats: 12g

12. Tangy Chicken Fillet

Ingredients:

14oz chicken fillet

3 tbsp orange marmalade

Grated zest and juice of 1 orange

1 tbsp white wine vinegar

Dash of Tabasco sauce

Salt and pepper

Sauce:

1 tbsp olive oil

1 small onion, chopped

1 small, green pepper, deseeded and thinly sliced

1 tbsp corn flour

5 fl oz orange juice

Serve with:

Cooked rice

Mixed salad leaves

Preparation:

Place a large piece of double thickness foil in a shallow dish. Put the chicken fillet in the center of the foil and season to taste.

Heat the marmalade, orange zest and juice, vinegar and Tabasco sauce in a small pan, stirring, until the marmalade melts and the ingredients combine. Pour the mixture over the chicken and wrap the meat in the foil. Seal the parcel well so that the juices cannot run out. Place over hot coals and barbecue for 25 minutes, turning the parcel occasionally.

For the sauce, heat the oil in a pan and cook the onion for 2-3 minutes. Add the pepper and cook for 3-4 minutes.

Remove the meat from the foil and place on the rack. Pour the juices into the pan with the sauce.

Continue barbecuing the chicken for another 10-20 minutes, turning, until cooked through and golden.

In a bowl, mix the cornflour into a paste with a little orange juice. Add to the sauce with the remaining cooking juices. Cook, stirring until it thickens. Slice the fillet, spoon over the sauce and serve with rice and salad leaves.

Nutrition information per serving: Kcal: 230 Protein: 19g, Carbs: 20g, Fats: 9g

13. Lemon Chicken Skewers

Ingredients:

4 chicken breasts, skinned and boned

1 tsp ground coriander

2 tsp lemon juice

10 fl oz natural yogurt

1 lemon

2 tbsp chopped fresh coriander

Oil, for brushing

Salt and pepper

Sprigs of fresh coriander, to garnish

Preparation:

Steps:

Cut the chicken into 2.5-cm/1-inch pieces and place them in a shallow, non-metallic dish.

Add the ground coriander, lemon juice, 4 tablespoons of the yogurt, and salt and pepper to taste. Mix together until thoroughly combined. Cover with cling film and chill for at least 2 hours, preferably overnight.

To make the lemon yogurt, peel and finely chop the lemon, discarding any pips. In a bowl, stir the lemon into the remaining yogurt along with the chopped coriander. Chill until required.

Thread the chicken pieces onto skewers. Brush the rack with oil, baste the skewers with it, then place them on the rack. Barbecue over hot coals for about 15 minutes, basting with the oil.

Transfer the cooked chicken kebabs to warm serving plates and garnish with sprigs of fresh coriander, lemon wedges, and fresh salad leaves. Serve the chicken with the lemon yogurt.

Nutrition information per serving: Kcal: 187 Protein: 34g, Carbs: 6g, Fats: 3g

14. Herb and Garlic Prawns

Ingredients:

12 oz raw prawns, peeled

2 tbsp chopped fresh parsley

4 tbsp lemon juice

4 tbsp olive oil

2 garlic cloves, chopped

Salt and pepper

Preparation:

Place the prepared prawns in a shallow, non-metallic dish with the parsley, lemon juice, and salt and pepper to taste. Leave the prawns to marinate in the herb mixture for at least 30 minutes.

Heat the oil with the garlic in a small saucepan. Stir to mix thoroughly.

Use a slotted spoon to remove the prawns from the marinade and add them to the pan containing the garlic. Stir the prawns into the garlic until well-coated, then thread them onto skewers.

Barbecue the kebabs over hot coals for 5-10 minutes, until the prawns turn pink and are cooked through. Brush the prawns with the remaining garlic during the cooking time.

Transfer the herb and garlic prawn kebabs to serving plates. Drizzle over any of the remaining garlic and serve at once.

Nutrition information per serving: Kcal: 160 Protein: 16g, Carbs: 1g, Fats: 9g

15. Tuna Steaks

Ingredients:

4 tuna steaks, about 6 oz each

½ tsp finely grated lime zest

1 garlic clove, crushed

2 tsp olive oil

1 tsp ground cumin

1 tsp ground coriander

Pepper

1 tbsp lime juice

Sprigs of fresh coriander, to garnish

Preparation:

Trim the skin from the tuna steaks, then rinse and pat dry with absorbent kitchen paper.

In a small bowl, mix together the lime zest, garlic, olive oil, cumin, ground coriander and pepper to make a paste.

Spread the paste thinly on both sides of the tuna. Cook the tuna steaks for 5 minutes, turning once, on a foil-covered barbecue rack over hot coals, or in an oiled, ridged grill pan over high heat, in batches if necessary. Cook for another 4-5 minutes, drain on kitchen paper and transfer to a serving plate.

Sprinkle the lime juice and sprigs of fresh coriander over the cooked fish. Serve the tuna steaks with avocado relish and wedges of lime and tomato.

Nutrition information per serving: Kcal: 239 Protein: 42g, Carbs: 0.5g, Fats: 8g

16. Vegetarian Chili Beans

Ingredients:

1 tbsp oil

2 cloves garlic, crushed

2 small fresh red chilies, finely chopped

1 green pepper, diced

14 oz red kidney beans, soaked

14 oz chopped tomatoes

4 oz tomato pasta sauce

1 teaspoon soft brown sugar

Preparation:

Heat the oil in a heavy-based pan and cook the garlic, chili and onion for 3 minutes, or until the onion is golden.

Add the remaining ingredients, bring to a boil, then reduce the heat to simmer for 15 minutes, or until thickened.

Nutrition information per serving: Kcal: 190 Protein: 9g, Carbs: 34g, Fats: 1.5g

17. Vegetable Strudel

Ingredients:

1 large eggplant

1 red pepper

3 zucchini, sliced lengthwise

2 tbsps olive oil

6 sheets filo pastry

1¾ oz baby English spinach leaves

2 oz feta cheese, sliced

Preparation:

Slice the eggplant lengthwise. Sprinkle with salt and leave for 20 minutes (to draw out the bitterness). Rinse well and pat dry.

Cut the pepper into large flat pieces and place, skin side up, under a hot grill until the skin blackens and blisters. Put in a plastic bag, then peel the skin away. Brush the eggplant and zucchini slices with some of the olive oil and grill for 5-10 minutes, or until golden brown. Set aside to cool. Preheat the oven to moderately hot 375ºF.

Brush one sheet of filo pastry at a time with olive oil then lay them on top of each other. Place half the eggplant slices lengthwise down the center of the filo and top with layers of zucchini, pepper, spinach and feta cheese. Repeat the layers until the vegetable and cheese are used up. Tuck in the ends of the pastry, then roll up like a parcel. Brush lightly with oil, place on a baking tray and bake for 35 minutes, or until golden brown.

Nutrition information per serving: Kcal: 287 Protein: 16g, Carbs: 38g, Fats: 4g

18. Hot Cheddar Salad

Ingredients:

¼ cup sweet chili sauce

1 tsp crushed garlic

1 tsp grated ginger

2 tbsp tomato sauce

1 lb firm Cheddar, cut into ½ inch cubes

2 tbsp oil

2 carrots, sliced

2 zucchini, sliced

6 spring onions, sliced

3½ oz sugar snap peas, topped and tailed

Preparation:

Mix the sweet chili sauce, garlic, ginger and tomato sauce in a bowl. Add the cheddar. Cover and marinate for 10 minutes.

Drain the cheddar, reserving the marinade. Heat half the oil in a large frying pan. Add the cheddar and cook the batches over high heat for 4 minutes, or until brown all over, turning often. Set aside.

Heat the remaining oil. Add the vegetables and toss over high heat for 2-3 minutes. Add the cheese and reserved marinade. Bring to a boil, stirring gently to combine the mixture. Remove from the heat and serve at once.

Nutrition information per serving: Kcal: 195 Protein: 4g, Carbs: 19g, Fats: 11g

19. Stuffed Field Mushrooms

Ingredients:

4 large field mushrooms

1 oz olive oil

1 leek, sliced

2-4 cloves garlic, crushed

2 tsp cumin seeds

1 tsp ground coriander

¼ - ½ tsp chili powder

2 tomatoes, chopped

2 cups mixed frozen vegetables

½ cup cooked brown rice

1/3 cup grated Cheddar

¼ cup grated Parmesan

¼ cup cashews, chopped

Preparation:

Preheat the oven to 400 degrees. Wipe the mushrooms

with a paper towel. Remove the stalks and chop them finely.

Heat up the oil in a pan. Add the chopped mushroom stalks and leek and cook for 2-3 minutes, or until soft. Mix in the garlic, cumin seeds, ground coriander and chili powder and cook for 1 minute, or until the mixture is fragrant.

Stir in the tomato and frozen vegetables. Bring to a boil, reduce the heat and simmer for 5 minutes. Stir in the rice and season well.

Spoon the mixture into the mushroom caps, sprinkle with the Cheddar and Parmesan and bake for 15 minutes, or until the cheese has melted. Scatter with the cashews and serve.

Nutrition information per serving: Kcal: 180 Protein: 3g, Carbs: 6g, Fats: 3.5g

20.   Lentil Masala Burgers

Ingredients:

1 cup red lentils

1 tbsp oil

2 onions, sliced

1 tsp ground cumin

1 tsp ground coriander

1 tsp garam masala

14 oz chickpeas, soaked

1 egg

¼ cup chopped fresh parsley

2 tbsp chopped fresh coriander

2¼ cups stale breadcrumbs

Plain flour, for dusting

Preparation:

Add the lentils to a large pan of boiling water and simmer for 15 minutes, or until tender. Drain well. Heat up the oil in a medium-sized skillet. Add the onion and stir-fry for 3 minutes, or until translucent and soft. Now add the spices and stir well. Remove from the heat and allow it to cool.

Transfer to a food processor. Add the chickpeas, egg, and half the lentils. Blend until smooth and transfer to a bowl. Add the remaining lentils, parsley, coriander and breadcrumbs. Mix well and divide into ten portions.

Using your hands, shape the round patties. Toss the patties in flour, shaking off the excess. Place on a lightly greased hot barbecue grill or hotplate. Cook for 3-4 minutes on each side, or until browned.

Nutrition information per serving: Kcal: 127 Protein: 15g, Carbs: 24g, Fats: 4g

21. Spicy Vegetable Couscous

Ingredients:

2 tbsp olive oil

2 cloves garlic, crushed

1 small red chili, diced

1 leek, thinly sliced

2 small fennel bulbs, sliced

2 tsp ground cumin

1 tsp ground coriander

1 tsp ground turmeric

1 tsp garam masala

11 oz sweet potato, chopped

2 parsnips, sliced

1½ cups vegetable stock

2 zucchini, thickly sliced

8 oz broccoli, cut into florets

2 tomatoes, peeled and chopped

1 red pepper, chopped

14 oz chickpeas, soaked

2 tbsp chopped fresh flat-leaf parsley

2 tbsp chopped fresh lemon thyme

Couscous:

1¼ cups instant couscous

2 tbsp olive oil

1 cup hot vegetable stock

Preparation:

Heat the oil in a large pan and add the garlic, chili, leek and fennel. Cook over medium heat for 10 minutes, or until the leek and fennel are soft and golden brown.

Add the cumin, coriander, turmeric, garam masala, sweet potato and parsnip. Cook for 5 minutes, stirring to coat the vegetables with spices.

Add the vegetable stock and simmer, covered, for 15 minutes. Stir in the zucchini, broccoli, tomato, pepper and chickpeas. Simmer, uncovered, for 30 minutes, or until the vegetables are tender. Stir in the herbs.

Put the couscous and olive oil in a bowl. Pour in the stock and leave to absorb for 5 minutes. Fluff gently with a fork to separate the grains. Make the couscous into a 'nest' on each plate and serve the spicy vegetables in the middle.

Nutrition information per serving: Kcal: 219 Protein: 6.5g, Carbs: 40g, Fats: 3g

22. Nut Roast

Ingredients:

2 tbsp olive oil

1 large onion, diced

2 cloves garlic, crushed

10 oz field mushrooms, finely chopped

6½ oz raw cashews

6½ oz Brazil nuts

1 cup grated Cheddar

¼ cup freshly grated Parmesan

1 egg, lightly beaten

2 tbsp chopped fresh chives

1 cup fresh wholemeal breadcrumbs

Tomato Sauce:

1 fl oz olive oil

1 onion, finely chopped

1 clove garlic, crushed

13 oz tomatoes, chopped

1 tbsp tomato paste

1 tsp caster sugar

Preparation:

Preheat the oven to 350 degrees.

Grease a 5½ x 8½ inch loaf tin and line the base with baking paper. Heat up the oil in a medium-sized skillet. Add onion and garlic. Stir-fry until soft. Now add mushrooms and continue to cook until the water evaporates. Remove from the heat and allow it to cool.

Place the nuts in a food processor and blend until finely chopped.

Combine the ingredients and press into the loaf tin. Bake for 15 minutes. Leave in the tin for 5 minutes.

For the sauce:

Heat up the oil in a frying pan, over a medium heat. Add onion and garlic and stir-fry for about five minutes. Now add the tomatoes, sugar, tomato paste, and 1/3 cup of water. Continue to cook for five more minutes.

Serve with sliced nut roast.

Nutrition information per serving: Kcal: 297 Protein: 12g, Carbs: 24g, Fats: 14g

23. Falafel

Ingredients:

2 cups chickpeas, soaked

1 small onion, chopped

2 cloves garlic, crushed

2 tbsp chopped fresh parsley

1 tbsp chopped fresh coriander

2 tsp ground cumin

½ tsp baking powder

Oil, for deep-frying

Hummus:

425g/14 oz can chickpeas

2-3 tbsp lemon juice

2 tbsp olive oil

2 cloves garlic, crushed

3 tbsp tahini

Tomato salsa:

2 tomatoes, peeled and finely chopped

¼ Lebanese cucumber, finely chopped

½ green pepper, finely chopped

2 tbsp chopped fresh parsley

1 tsp sugar

2 tsp chili sauce

Grated rind and juice of 1 lemon

Preparation:

Soak the chickpeas in 3 cups water for at least 4 hours. Drain and mix in a food processor for 30 seconds, or until finely ground.

Add the onion, garlic, parsley, coriander, cumin, baking powder and 1 tbsp water, and process for 10 seconds, or until the mixture forms a rough paste. Cover and set aside for 30 minutes.

To make the hummus, place the drained chickpeas, lemon juice, oil and garlic in a food processor. Season and process for 20-30 seconds, or until smooth. Add the tahini and process for a further 10 seconds.

To make the tomato salsa, mix together all the ingredients and season with plenty of freshly ground black pepper.

Shape heaped tablespoons of the falafel mixture into balls. Squeeze out the excess moisture. Heat the oil in a deep, heavy-based pan, until a cube of bread browns in 15 seconds. Lower the falafel into the oil in batches of five. Cook for 3-4 minutes each batch. When well-browned, remove with a large slotted spoon. Drain on paper towels and serve hot or cold with Lebanese bread, hummus and tomato salsa.

Nutrition information per serving: Kcal: 114 Protein: 4g, Carbs: 10g, Fats: 6g

24. Vegetable Frittata

Ingredients:

1 tbsp olive oil

2 cloves garlic, crushed

1 small red onion, chopped

1 small red pepper, chopped

1 lb roasted, boiled or steamed potatoes, thickly sliced

¼ cup chopped fresh parsley

6 eggs, lightly beaten

¼ cup grated Parmesan

Preparation:

Heat the oil in a large, heavy-based, non-stick frying pan. Add the garlic, onion, and pepper and stir over medium heat for 2-3 minutes. Add the potato slices and cook for 2-3 minutes more. Stir in the parsley and spread the mixture evenly in the pan.

Beat the eggs with 2 tbsp water, pour into the pan and cook over medium heat for 15 minutes, without burning the base.

Preheat the grill to high. Sprinkle the Parmesan over the frittata and grill for a few minutes to cook the egg and lightly brown. Cut into wedges to serve.

Nutrition information per serving: Kcal: 208 Protein: 11g, Carbs: 17g, Fats: 10g

25. Grated Vegetable Frittata

Ingredients:

3 tbsp olive oil

1 onion, finely chopped

1 small carrot, grated

1 small zucchini, grated

1 cup grated pumpkin

1/3 cup finely diced Cheddar cheese

5 eggs, lightly beaten

Preparation

Heat 2 tablespoons of the oil in a pan and cook the onion for 5 minutes, or until soft. Add the carrot, zucchini, and pumpkin and cook over low heat, covered, for 3 minutes. Transfer to a bowl and allow to cool. Stir in the cheese and plenty of salt and pepper. Add the eggs.

Heat the remaining oil in a small non-stick frying pan. Add the frittata mixture and shake the pan to spread it evenly. Reduce to low and cook for 15-20 minutes, or until set almost all the way through. Tilt the pan and lift the edges occasionally to allow the uncooked egg to flow underneath. Brown the top under a preheated hot grill. Cut into wedges and serve immediately.

Nutrition information per serving: Kcal: 166 Protein: 114g, Carbs: 6g, Fats: 5g

Dinner Recipes

26. Vegetarian Sausages

Ingredients:

1 tbsp sunflower oil

1 small onion, finely chopped

1¾ oz mushrooms, finely chopped

½ red pepper, deseeded and finely chopped

14 oz canned cannellini beans, rinsed and drained

3½ oz fresh breadcrumbs

3½ oz Cheddar cheese, grated

1 tsp dried mixed herbs

1 egg yolk

Seasoned plain flour, to coat

Oil, for cooking

Preparation:

Heat the oil in a pan and cooked the prepared onion,

mushrooms, and red pepper until softened.

Mash the cannellini beans in a large mixing bowl. Add the chopped onion, mushroom, and red pepper mixture, and the breadcrumbs, cheese, herbs and egg yolk, and mix together well.

Press the mixture together with your fingers and shape into eight (8) sausages.

Roll each sausage in the seasoned flour. Chill for at least 30 minutes.

Barbecue the sausages on a sheet of oiled foil set over medium-hot coals for 15-20 minutes, turning and basting frequently with oil, until golden.

Split the bread rolls down the middle and insert a layer of fried onions. Place the sausages in the rolls and serve.

Nutrition information per serving: Kcal: 213 Protein: 8g, Carbs: 19g, Fats: 12g

27. Colorful Kebabs

Ingredients:

1 red pepper, deseeded

1 yellow pepper, deseeded

1 green pepper, deseeded

1 small onion

8 cherry tomatoes

3½ oz wild mushrooms

Seasoned oil:

6 tbsp olive oil

1 garlic clove, crushed

½ tsp mixed dried herbs

Preparation:

Cut the red, yellow and green peppers into 1-inch pieces.

Peel the onion and cut into wedges, leaving the root end just intact to help keep the wedges together.

Thread the pepper pieces, onion wedges, tomatoes, and

mushrooms onto skewers, alternating the colors of the peppers.

To make the seasoned oil, mix together the olive oil, garlic and mixed herbs in a small bowl. Brush the mixture liberally over the kebabs.

Barbecue the kebabs over medium-hot coals for 10-15 minutes, brushing with the seasoned oil and turning the skewers frequently.

Transfer the vegetable kebabs onto warmed serving plates. Serve the kebabs immediately, accompanied by a rich walnut sauce (see Tip below).

Nutrition information per serving: Kcal: 131 Protein: 2g, Carbs: 8g, Fats: 11g

28. Garlic Potato Wedges

Ingredients:

3 large baking potatoes, scrubbed

4 tbsp olive oil

2 garlic cloves, chopped

1 tbsp chopped fresh rosemary

1 tbsp chopped fresh parsley

1 tbsp chopped fresh thyme

Salt and pepper

Preparation:

Bring a large saucepan of water to a boil, add the potatoes and parboil them for 10 minutes. Drain the potatoes, refresh under cold water and then drain them again thoroughly.

Transfer the potatoes to a chopping board. When cold enough to handle, cut into thick wedges, but do not peel.

Heat the oil and garlic in a small saucepan. Cook gently until the garlic begins to brown, then remove the pan from the heat.

Stir the herbs, and salt and pepper to taste, into the mixture in the saucepan.

Brush the warm garlic and herb mixture generously over the parboiled potato wedges.

Barbecue the potatoes over hot coals for 10-15 minutes, brushing liberally with any of the remaining garlic and herb mixture, or until the potato wedges are just tender.

Transfer the garlic potato wedges to a warm serving plate and serve as a starter or side dish.

Nutrition information per serving: Kcal: 257 Protein: 3g, Carbs: 26g, Fats: 16g

29. Spiced Pilaf with Saffron

Ingredients:

Large pinch of good quality saffron threads

16 fl oz boiling water

1 tsp salt

2 tbsp flaxseed oil

2 tbsp olive oil

1 large onion, very finely chopped

3 tbsp pine kernels

12 oz long grain rice (not basmati)

2oz sultanas

6 green cardamom pods, shells lightly cracked

6 cloves

Pepper

Very finely chopped fresh coriander or flat-leaved parsley, to garnish

Preparation:

Toast the saffron threads in a dry frying pan over a medium heat, stirring, for 2 minutes, until they give off an aroma. Immediately tip out onto a plate.

Pour the boiling water into a measuring jug, stir in the saffron and salt and leave to infuse for 30 minutes.

Heat up the oil in a frying pan over a medium-high heat. Add the onion. Cook for about 5 minutes, stirring.

Lower the heat, stir the pine kernels into the onions and continue cooking for 2 minutes, stirring, until the nuts just begin to turn a golden color. Be careful not to burn them.

Stir in the rice, coating all the grains with oil. Stir for 1 minute, then add the sultanas, cardamom pods, and cloves. Pour in the saffron-flavored water and bring to a boil. Lower the heat, cover, and simmer for 15 minutes without removing the lid.

Remove from the heat. Leave to stand for 5 minutes without uncovering. Remove the lid and check that the rice is tender, the liquid has been absorbed and the surface has small indentations all over.

Fluff up the rice and adjust the seasoning. Stir in the herbs and serve.

Nutrition information per serving: Kcal: 347 Protein: 5g, Carbs: 60g, Fats: 11g

30. Indian Charred Chicken

Ingredients:

4 chicken breasts, skinned and boned

2 tbsp curry paste

1 tbsp sunflower oil, plus extra for cooking

1 tbsp brown sugar

1 tsp ground ginger

½ tsp ground cumin

Cucumber Raita:

¼ cucumber

Salt

5 fl oz low-fat natural yogurt

¼ tsp chili powder

Preparation:

Place the chicken breasts between two sheets of baking paper or clingfilm. Pound them with the flat side of a meat mallet or rolling pin to flatten them.

Mix together the curry paste, oil, brown sugar, ginger and

cumin in a small bowl. Spread the mixture over both sides of the chicken and then set aside until required.

To make the raita, peel the cucumber and scoop out the seeds with a spoon. Grate the cucumber flesh, sprinkle with salt, place in a sieve and leave to stand for 10 minutes. Rinse off the salt and squeeze out any remaining moisture by pressing the cucumber with the base of a glass or the back of a spoon.

In a small bowl, mix the grated cucumber with the natural yogurt and stir in the chili powder. Leave to chill until needed.

Transfer the chicken pieces to an oiled rack and barbecue over hot coals for 10 minutes, turning once.

Warm the naan bread at the side of the barbecue.

Serve the chicken with the naan bread and cucumber raita, accompanied by fresh salad leaves.

Nutrition information per serving: Kcal: 228 Protein: 28g, Carbs: 12g, Fats: 8g

31. Stuffed Apples

Ingredients:

4 medium cooking apples

2 tbsp chopped walnuts

2 tbsp ground almonds

2 tbsp light muscovado sugar

2 tbsp chopped cherries

2 tbsp chopped crystallized ginger

4 tbsp flaxseed oil

Single cream or thick natural yogurt, to serve

Preparation:

Core the apples and, using a sharp knife, score each one around the middle to prevent the apple skins from splitting during barbecuing.

To make the filling, in a small bowl, mix together the walnuts, almonds, sugar, cherries and ginger.

Spoon the filling mixture into each apple, pushing it down into the hollowed-out core. Mound a little of the filling mixture on top of each apple.

Place each apple on a large square of double-thickness foil and generously dot with the oil. Wrap up the foil so that each apple is completely enclosed.

Barbecue the parcels containing the apples over hot coals for about 25-30 minutes, or until tender.

Transfer the apples to warm individual serving plates. Serve with lashings of whipped single cream or thick natural yogurt.

Nutrition information per serving: Kcal: 294 Protein: 3g, Carbs: 31g, Fats: 18g

32. Barbecued Bananas

Ingredients:

4 bananas

2 passionfruit

4 tbsp orange juice

4 tbsp orange-flavored extract

Orange flavored cream:

5 fl oz double cream

3 tbsp icing sugar

2 tbsp orange flavored extract

Preparation:

To make the orange-flavored cream, pour the double cream into a mixing bowl and sprinkle over the icing sugar. Whisk the mixture until it is standing in soft peaks. Carefully fold in the orange-flavored extract and chill in the refrigerator until needed.

Peel the bananas and place each one onto a sheet of foil.

Cut the passion fruit in half and squeeze the juice of each

half over each banana. Spoon over the orange juice and extract.

Fold the foil carefully over the top of the bananas so that they are completely enclosed.

Place the parcels on a baking tray and cook over hot coals for 10-15 minutes, or until they are just tender (test by inserting a cocktail stick or a toothpick).

Transfer the foil parcels to warm, individual serving plates. Open out the foil parcels and then serve immediately with the orange-flavored cream.

Nutrition information per serving: Kcal: 380 Protein: 2g, Carbs: 43g, Fats: 11g

33. Easy Chicken Wraps

Ingredients:

7oz chicken breast, boneless and skinless, chopped into bite-sized pieces

2 cups of chicken broth

1 cup of fat-free Greek yogurt

½ cup of fresh parsley, chopped

½ tsp of sea salt

¼ tsp of ground pepper

1 tbsp of oregano

1 small tomato, finely chopped

1 small onion, finely chopped

4 corn tortillas

Preparation:

Combine chicken broth and chicken meat in a deep pot. Bring it to a boil. Reduce the heat to medium and continue to cook for about 10-15 minutes.

Remove from the heat and cool for a while.

In a large bowl, combine Greek yogurt, chicken meat, parsley, salt, and pepper. Mix gently until the chicken is well coated.

Spread this mixture over tortillas and top add finely chopped tomato, onion, and some oregano.

Roll and serve.

Nutrition information per serving: Kcal: 167, Protein: 21g, Carbs: 14.5g, Fats: 5g

34. Homemade Tomato Soup

Ingredients:

2oz tomato, peeled and roughly chopped

Ground black pepper to taste

1 tbsp of celery, finely chopped

1 onion, diced

1 tbsp of fresh basil, finely chopped

Fresh water

Preparation:

Preheat the non-stick frying pan over a medium-high temperature. Add the onions, celery, and fresh basil. Sprinkle some pepper and stir-fry for about 10 minutes, until caramelized.

Add the tomato and about ¼ cup of water. Reduce the heat to minimum and cook for about 15 minutes, until softened. Now add about 1 cup of water and bring it to a boil. Remove from the heat and serve with fresh parsley.

Nutrition information per serving: Kcal: 21 Protein: 0.7g, Carbs: 4.9g, Fats: 0.9g

35. Chunky Corn Wraps

Ingredients:

4 lettuce leaves

4 tbsp of sweet corn

4 tbsp of red beans

1 small tomato, finely chopped

4 tbsp of tuna, oil free

0,7oz grated Gouda cheese

½ tsp of sea salt

4 corn tortillas

Preparation:

In a small bowl, combine the tuna with sweet corn, red beans, grated gouda, and finely chopped tomato.

Heat up tortillas in a microwave for about a minute. Spread some of the mixture on each tortilla, add lettuce and wrap. Secure with toothpicks.

Nutrition information per serving: Kcal: 185, Protein: 29g, Carbs: 21g, Fats: 7g

36. Sweet Potato and Salmon Patties

Ingredients:

1lb sweet potato, sliced

1lb fresh salmon fillet

2 cups of milk

2 eggs

1 tsp of sea salt

1 tbsp of flaxseed oil

1 cup of all-purpose flour

½ cup of breadcrumbs

½ cup of parsley, finely chopped

Vegetable oil

Preparation:

Place the potato in a deep pot. Add enough water to cover and bring it to a boil. Cook until soft. Remove from the heat and transfer to a bowl. Add one teaspoon of salt, milk, and oil. Mash until the smooth puree. Set aside.

Finely chop the salmon fillet and combine with sweet

potato puree. Add flour, eggs, and parsley. Mix until well combined. Using your hands, shape 1-inch thick patties and coat in breadcrumbs.

Preheat some oil over a medium-high heat. Fry each patty for about 2-3 minutes on each side.

Nutrition information per serving: Kcal: 325, Protein: 45g, Carbs: 41g, Fats: 16g

37. English muffins

Ingredients:

1 cup of unbleached all - purpose flour

¼ cup of brown sugar

¼ tsp of sea salt

1 tsp of yeast

1 tbsp of organic almond butter, melted

2 cups of milk

Preparation:

Combine dry ingredients in a large bowl and mix well. Now gently stir in 1 tbsp of melted almond butter and milk, until the dough forms a ball. You can add some more milk to get the right consistency. Mix well for few minutes, using your hands or an electric mixer. The dough will become very sticky. Now add some more flour (2 tbsp should be enough) to get a nice and smooth mixture. Cover and let it rise for about 15 minutes.

Meanwhile, preheat the oven to 350 degrees. Use a muffin molds to shape your muffins. Bake for about 20 minutes, until nice gold brown color.

Nutrition information per serving: Kcal: 287, Protein: 24g, Carbs: 29g, Fats: 14g

38. Pumpkin pancakes

Ingredients:

5 egg whites

½ tablespoon cinnamon

¼ cup oats

sugar

1 tablespoon of ground flax

1/3 cup of canned or mashed fresh pumpkin

Preparation:

Mix all the ingredients together well. Now, heat the frying pan until it's fully hot. Don't keep it on high temperature. Let it get hot on medium temperature and keep it the same throughout. Use a big spoon to put the blended ingredients on the frying pan. Basically, this is the easiest part. You simply have to make pancakes now the usual way.

Nutrition information per serving: Kcal: 198, Protein: 28g, Carbs: 31g, Fats: 14g

39. Fruit mix

Ingredients

1/3 cup of blueberries (frozen recommended)

half a cup of orange juice

1 ½ cups of plain yogurt

1 cup of hulled strawberries

1 or 2 bananas

ice crush if required

and one tablespoon of honey

How to Prepare:

Put all the ingredients in the blender jug and blend them until the blend is smooth. If necessary, add a little more orange juice.

Nutrition information per serving: Kcal: 89, Protein: 8g, Carbs: 17g, Fats: 3g

40. "Nori Sushi"

Ingredients:

<u>Rice:</u>

1 and 3/4 cups peeled fresh parnsips

3 tbsp of macadamia nuts, minced

3 tbsp of pine nuts, minced

1 tbsp flax or hemp seed oil

1 ½ tbsp of agave nectar

2 tbsp of lemon juice

1-2 pinches of Celtic sea salt

1 tbsp of south river miso

1 avocado

½ cup of sprouts (ginger sprouts, sunflower sprouts)

<u>Sushi:</u>

1 medium carrot

1 red bell pepper

1 stalk celery

1 scallion

1 cucumber

1 yellow zucchini

Marinade:

3 tbs sesame oil

1 tbs black sesame seeds

2 pinches of salt

2 tbsp of lemon juice

Preparation:
Spread 2-3 tbs of the rice mixture on the nori sheet. Put 1-2 tbs of the marinated veggies on top. Spread that with a few pieces of the avocado. Take sprouts and place it on the avocado and the rice. You can roll the sushi with a sushi mat or use your fingers. Using a knife cut the nori roll into 5-6 equal parts.
Plate 5 nori rolls and garnish the platter with garlic chives and sesame seeds.

Nutrition information per serving: Kcal: 254, Protein: 36g, Carbs: 45g, Fats: 17g

Snacks:

41. Walnut and Strawberries Salad

Ingredients:

½ cup of ground walnuts

2 cups of fresh strawberries

1 tbsp of strawberry syrup

2 tbsp of nonfat cream

1 tbsp of brown sugar

Preparation:

Wash and cut the strawberries into small pieces. Mix with ground walnuts in a bowl. In a separate bowl, combine strawberry syrup, nonfat cream, and brown sugar. Beat well with a fork and use to top the salad.

Nutrition information per serving: Kcal: 180, Protein: 29g, Carbs: 27g, Fats: 19g

42. Creamy beans

Ingredients:

1 cup of green beans, cooked

1 medium tomato

1.5 cup of cottage cheese

1 tsp of garlic sauce

1 tbsp of flaxseed oil

salt and pepper to taste

Preparation:

Soak the beans in water for 30 minutes. Remove and wash. Cut the tomato into small pieces and mix with other ingredients. Season with salt and pepper. Serve cold.

Nutrition information per serving: Kcal: 197, Protein: 40g, Carbs: 38g, Fats: 21g

43. Grated Red Cabbage Side Dish

Ingredients:

1 cup of grated red cabbage

½ cup of grated carrot

½ cup of grated beetroot

1 cup of feta cheese

3 tbsp of minced almonds

1 tbsp of almond extract

1 tbsp of almond oil

salt to taste

Preparation:

Mix the vegetables in a large bowl. Add feta cheese, minced almonds and almond extract. Season with almond oil and salt. You can add some lemon juice or vinegar, but that is optional.

Nutrition information per serving: Kcal: 186, Protein: 36g, Carbs: 45g, Fats: 17g

44. Spicy green beans

Ingredients:

½ cup of green beans, cooked

1 large tomato

1 cup of chopped radicchio

2 cups of tuna, without oil

1 tbsp of tomato sauce

1 tsp of ground chili

½ tsp of pepper

½ tsp of tabasco sauce

1 tbsp of olive oil

salt to taste

Preparation:

First, you want to prepare a spicy sauce. Mix tomato sauce with ground chili, pepper, and tabasco sauce until smooth mixture (you can add few drops of lemon juice, but that is optional). Wash and cut tomato, combine with other ingredients and spicy sauce. Season with olive oil and salt.

Nutrition information per serving: Kcal: 232, Protein: 31g, Carbs: 45g, Fats: 17g

45. Spring Arugula

Ingredients:

1 large tomato

1 small onion

1 tbsp of ground garlic

1 cup of chopped arugula

1 cup of cottage cheese

1 tbsp of lemon juice

salt and pepper to taste

Preparation:

Wash and cut the vegetables. Combine the ingredients in a large bowl and season with lemon juice, salt, and pepper.

You can add some chili, curry, turmeric or ginger, depending on your taste. This is optional.

Nutrition information per serving: Kcal: 10 Protein: 2g, Carbs: 3g, Fats: 0g

46. Quinoa and Cheese

Ingredients:

1/3 cup of quinoa

1 cup of chopped radish

½ cup of grated cabbage

½ cup of feta cheese

olive oil

salt to taste

Preparation:

First, you want to cook the quinoa. To cook one cup of quinoa, you need two cups of water. It takes about 20 minutes, on a low temperature to cook quinoa. Remove from the heat and drain. Allow it to cool for a while.

Mix the quinoa with chopped radish and grated cabbage. Add feta cheese, olive oil, and a little salt.

Nutrition information per serving: Kcal: 204 Protein: 13g, Carbs: 18g, Fats: 9g

JUICES

1. Banana Beet Juice

Ingredients:

1 large banana, sliced

1 whole beet, trimmed

1 cup blackberries

1 small green apple, chopped

¼ tsp cinnamon, ground

1 oz water

Preparation:

Peel the banana and cut into thin slices. Set aside.

Wash the beet and trim off the green ends. Slightly peel and cut into small pieces. Set aside.

Place the blackberries in a colander and rinse well under cold running water. Slightly drain and set aside.

Wash the apple and cut in half. Remove the core and cut into bite-sized pieces. Set aside.

Now, combine blackberries, banana, beet, and apple in a

juicer and process until well juiced. Transfer to a serving glass and stir in the cinnamon and water.

Refrigerate for about 10-15 minutes and serve.

Nutritional information per serving: Kcal: 233, Protein: 5.4g, Carbs: 72.3g, Fats: 1.6g

2. Carrot Mango Juice

Ingredients:

1 large carrot, sliced

1 cup mango, chunked

2 whole apricots, pitted

1 cup cauliflower, chopped

1 cup kale, torn

¼ tsp ginger, ground

Preparation:

Wash and peel the carrot. Cut into thin slices and set aside.

Wash the mango and cut into small chunks. Fill the measuring cup and reserve the rest for later.

Wash the apricots and cut lengthwise in half. Remove the pits and cut into small pieces. Set aside.

Rinse the cauliflower and roughly chop it. Set aside.

Rinse the kale under cold running water. Slightly drain and roughly chop it. Set aside.

Now, combine carrot, mango, apricots, cauliflower, and

kale in a juicer and process until well juiced.

Transfer to a serving glass and stir in the water and ginger. Add some ice and serve immediately.

Nutritional information per serving: Kcal: 149, Protein: 4.4g, Carbs: 42.5g, Fats: 1.3g

3. Mango Plum Juice

Ingredients:

1 cup mango, chunked

3 whole plums, pitted

1 whole kiwi, peeled

1 whole guava, peeled

1 oz water

1 tbsp liquid honey

Preparation:

Peel the mango and cut into chunks. Set aside.

Wash the plums and cut in half. Remove the pits and cut into bite-sized pieces. Set aside.

Peel the kiwi and cut lengthwise in half. Set aside.

Peel the guava and cut into small pieces. Set aside.

Now, combine mango, plums, kiwi, and guava in a juicer. Process until well juiced. Transfer to a serving glass and stir in the water and honey.

Serve immediately.

Nutritional information per serving: Kcal: 286, Protein: 4.9g, Carbs: 65.3g, Fats: 2.1g

4. Strawberry Apple Juice

Ingredients:

2 medium-sized strawberries, chopped

1 small Golden Delicious apple, cored

1 cup pumpkin, chopped

1 cup apricots, sliced

1 tbsp liquid honey

Preparation:

Wash the strawberries and cut into bite-sized pieces. Set aside.

Wash the apple and remove the core. Cut into small chunks and set aside.

Peel the pumpkin and cut in half. Scoop out the seeds using a spoon. Cut one large wedge and peel it. Cut into small chunks and fill the measuring cup. Reserve the rest for later.

Wash the apricots and cut each in half. Remove the pits and thinly slice. Set aside.

Now, combine strawberries, apple pumpkin, and apricots

in a juicer and process until juiced. Transfer to a serving glass and stir in the honey.

Add some ice and serve.

Nutritional information per serving: Kcal: 222, Protein: 4g, Carbs: 62.3g, Fats: 1.1g

5. Banana Pineapple Juice

Ingredients:

1 large banana, sliced

1 cup pineapple, chunked

1 large pear, chopped

1 whole lemon, peeled

5 cherries, pitted

1 tbsp honey

Preparation:

Peel the banana and cut into small chunks. Set aside.

Cut the top of a pineapple and peel it using a sharp paring knife. Cut into small chunks and fill the measuring cup. Reserve the rest in a refrigerator.

Wash the pear and cut in half. Remove the core and cut into bite-sized pieces. Set aside.

Peel the lemon and cut lengthwise in half. Set aside.

Wash the cherries and cut each in half. Remove the pits and set aside.

Now, combine banana, pineapple, pear, lemon, and cherries in a juicer and process until juiced. Transfer to a serving glass and stir in the honey.

Refrigerate for 10 minutes before serving.

Nutritional information per serving: Kcal: 374, Protein: 4.3g, Carbs: 109g, Fats: 1.2g

6. Spicy Green Juice

Ingredients:

1 cup cabbage, shredded

1 cup fresh parsley, torn

1 cup spinach, torn

1 cup fresh kale, torn

1 cup cucumber, sliced

1 cup avocado, chunked

¼ tsp turmeric, ground

Preparation:

Wash the cabbage thoroughly and shred the cabbage. Fill the measuring cup and reserve the rest for later.

Combine spinach, kale, and parsley in a large colander. Rinse all under cold running water and slightly drain. Torn with hands and set aside.

Wash the cucumber and cut into thin slices. Set aside.

Peel the avocado and cut in half. Remove the pit and cut into small chunks. Fill the measuring cup and reserve the rest for later.

Now, combine cabbage, cucumber, spinach, kale, parsley, and avocado in a juicer and process until juiced. Transfer to a serving glass and stir in the turmeric.

Refrigerate for 20 minutes and serve.

Nutritional information per serving: Kcal: 272, Protein: 10.9g, Carbs: 33.1g, Fats: 23.5g

7. Mango Mint Juice

Ingredients:

1 cup fresh cherries

1 cup mango, chunked

1 cup fresh mint, torn

1 small apple, cored

¼ tsp ginger, ground

Preparation:

Peel the mango and cut into small chunks. Fill the measuring cup and refrigerate the rest for later.

Wash the mint thoroughly under cold running water. Slightly drain and torn with hands. Set aside.

Wash the cherries and cut each in half. Remove the pits and fill the measuring cup. Reserve the rest for some other juice.

Wash the apple and cut in half. Remove the core and cut into bite-sized pieces. Set aside.

Now, combine mango, mint, cherries, and apple in a juicer and process until juiced. Transfer to a serving glass and stir in the ginger.

Add some ice or refrigerate for 10 minutes before serving.

Nutritional information per serving: Kcal: 262, Protein: 4.3g, Carbs: 75.3g, Fats: 6.6g

8. Kiwi Apple Juice

Ingredients:

1 whole kiwi, sliced

1 small apple, cored

1 cup beets, sliced

1 small pear, cored

¼ tsp cinnamon, ground

2 oz water

Preparation:

Wash the beets and trim off the green ends. Peel and cut into thin slices. Fill the measuring cup and reserve the rest for some other juice.

Peel the kiwi and cut lengthwise in half. Set aside.

Wash the apple and pear. Remove the core and cut into bite-sized pieces. Set aside.

Now, combine kiwi, apple, beets, and pear in a juicer and process until well juiced. Transfer to a serving glass and stir in the cinnamon and water. Refrigerate for 10 minutes before serving.

Enjoy!

Nutritional information per serving: Kcal: 211, Protein: 4.2g, Carbs: 65.3g, Fats: 1.1g

9. Peach Lime Juice

Ingredients:

1 cup cantaloupe, diced

1 cup mango, chunked

1 medium-sized peach, pitted

1 whole lime, peeled

1 cup fresh mint, finely chopped

Preparation:

Wash the peach and cut lengthwise in half. Remove the pit and cut into bite-sized pieces. Set aside.

Peel the lime and cut lengthwise in half. Set aside.

Cut the cantaloupe in half. Scoop out the seeds and cut two wedges and peel them. Chop into chunks and set aside. Reserve the rest of the cantaloupe in a refrigerator.

Wash and peel the mango. Cut into small chunks and set aside.

Now, combine peach, lime, cantaloupe, mango, and mint in a juicer. Process until well juiced. Transfer to a serving glass and add some crushed ice.

Serve immediately.

Nutritional information per serving: Kcal: 205, Protein: 5.2g, Carbs: 59.2g, Fats: 1.6g

10. Kiwi Orange Juice

Ingredients:

1 whole kiwi, peeled

1 medium-sized orange, peeled

1 cup crookneck squash

1 cup fresh kale, torn

1 tbsp liquid honey

1 oz water

Preparation:

Peel the kiwi and cut lengthwise in half. Set aside.

Peel the orange and divide into wedges. Set aside.

Peel the crookneck squash and scrape out the seeds with a spoon. Cut into small cubes and fill the measuring cup. Reserve the rest of the squash for some other recipe. Wrap in a plastic foil and refrigerate.

Rinse the kale under cold running water and slightly drain. Torn with hands and set aside.

Now, combine kiwi, orange, crookneck squash, and kale in a juicer. Process until well juiced and transfer to a serving glass.

Stir in the honey and water. Add some ice before serving and enjoy!

Nutritional information per serving: Kcal: 126, Protein: 6.2g, Carbs: 36.3g, Fats: 1.5g

11. Orange Carrot Juice

Ingredients:

1 cup pineapple chunks

1 medium-sized orange, peeled

1 small carrot, chopped

1 whole lime, peeled

1 tbsp liquid honey

Preparation:

Cut the top of a pineapple and peel it using a sharp knife. Cut into small chunks. Reserve the rest of the pineapple in a refrigerator.

Peel the orange and divide into wedges. Cut each wedge in half and set aside.

Peel the carrot and cut into thin slices. Set aside.

Peel the lime and cut lengthwise in half. Set aside.

Now, combine orange, carrot, pineapple, and lime in a juicer and process until well juiced. Transfer to a serving glass and stir in the honey.

Refrigerate for 10 minutes before serving.

Nutritional information per serving: Kcal: 207, Protein: 2.7g, Carbs: 61.5g, Fats: 0.7g

12. Banana Lime Juice

Ingredients:

1 cup blueberries

1 medium-sized banana, chopped

1 whole lime, peeled

1 large pear, chopped

1 cup blackberries

1 large orange, wedged

Preparation:

Peel the banana and chop into chunks. Set aside.

Peel the lime and cut lengthwise in half. Set aside.

In a large colander, combine blueberries and blackberries. Rinse well under cold running water and drain. Set aside.

Wash the pear and cut in half. Remove the core and cut into bite-sized pieces. Set aside.

Peel the orange and divide into wedges. Set aside.

Now, combine banana, lime, blueberries, blackberries, pear, and orange in a juicer and process until well juiced.

Transfer to a serving glass and add some crushed ice.

Enjoy!

Nutritional information per serving: Kcal: 376, Protein: 7.2g, Carbs: 122.6g, Fats: 2.6g

13. Lemon Broccoli Juice

Ingredients:

1 whole lemon, peeled

1 cup of broccoli, chopped

2 large beets, trimmed and chopped

1 large cucumber, sliced

Preparation:

Peel the lemon and cut lengthwise in half. Set aside.

Wash the broccoli and cut into bite-sized pieces. Fill the measuring cup and reserve the rest for later.

Wash the beets and trim off the green parts. Cut into bite-sized pieces and set aside.

Wash the cucumber and cut into thin slices. Set aside.

Now, combine beets, lemon, broccoli, and cucumber in a juicer and process until juiced. Transfer to a serving glass and add some ice before serving.

Enjoy!

Nutritional information per serving: Kcal: 123, Protein: 7.8g, Carbs: 38.1g, Fats: 1.1g

14. Green Celery Kiwi Juice

Ingredients:

3 medium-sized celery stalks, chopped

2 large kiwis, peeled

1 medium-sized artichoke, chopped

¼ tsp ginger, ground

1 tbsp liquid honey

1 oz water

Preparation:

Trim off the outer leaves of the artichoke using a sharp paring knife. Wash it and cut into bite-sized pieces. Set aside.

Peel the ginger slice and cut into small pieces. Set aside.

Wash the celery stalks and cut into bite-sized pieces. Set aside.

Peel the kiwis and cut lengthwise in half. Set aside.

Now, combine artichoke, celery, and kiwi in a juicer. Process until well juiced and transfer to a serving glass. Stir in the honey, celery, and water. Refrigerate for 10 minutes before serving.

Enjoy!

Nutritional information per serving: Kcal: 174, Protein: 6.6g, Carbs: 54.6g, Fats: 1.2g

15. Orange Grape Juice

Ingredients:

1 large orange, wedged

1 cup green grapes

2 whole apricots, pitted

1 small ginger slice, peeled

1 oz water

Preparation:

Peel the orange and divide into wedges. Set aside.

Rinse the grapes under running water and set aside.

Wash the apricots and cut lengthwise in half. Remove the pits and cut into bite-sized pieces. Set aside.

Peel the ginger slice and cut into small pieces. Set aside.

Now, combine orange, grapes, apricots, and ginger in a juicer. Process until juiced and transfer to a serving glass. Add some ice before serving.

Enjoy!

Nutritional information per serving: Kcal: 157, Protein: 3.3g, Carbs: 45.7g, Fats: 0.8g

16. Banana Lime Juice

Ingredients:

1 large banana, chunked

1 large lime, peeled

2 cups cherries, pitted

2 large green apples, chopped

¼ tsp cinnamon

1 oz water

Preparation:

Peel the banana and chop into chunks. Set aside.

Peel the lime and cut lengthwise in half. Set aside.

Rinse the cherries under cold running water and drain. Cut each in half and remove the pits. Set aside.

Wash the apples and cut lengthwise in half. Remove the core and cut into small chunks.

Now, combine banana, lime, cherries, and apples in a juicer and process until well juiced.

Transfer to a serving glass and stir in the cinnamon and

water. Add some ice before serving and enjoy!

Nutritional information per serving: Kcal: 297, Protein: 4.2g, Carbs: 87.5g, Fats: 1.2g

17. Blueberry Strawberry Juice

Ingredients:

1 cup blueberries

3 large strawberries, chopped

1 cup blackberries

1 large lime, peeled

1 large cucumber, chopped

1 cup fresh mint, torn

2 oz water

Preparation:

Combine blueberries and blackberries in a colander. Rinse under cold running water and drain. Set aside.

Wash the strawberries and remove the stems, if any. Cut into bite-sized pieces and set aside.

Peel the lime and cut lengthwise in half. Set aside.

Wash the cucumber and cut into small chunks. Set aside.

Wash the mint and torn with hands. Set aside.

Now, combine blueberries, blackberries, strawberries,

cucumber, and mint in a juicer and process until juiced. Transfer to serving glasses and stir in the water.

Add some ice or refrigerate for 10 minutes before serving.

Nutritional information per serving: Kcal: 173, Protein: 6.6g, Carbs: 57.8g, Fats: 1.9g

18. Mango Orange Juice

Ingredients:

1 cup mango, chunked

1 small orange, peeled

1 large carrot, sliced

1 cup fresh mint, torn

1 oz coconut water

1 tbsp liquid honey

Preparation:

Peel the mango and cut into small chunks. Set aside.

Peel the orange and divide into wedges. Cut each wedge in half and set aside.

Wash the carrot and slightly peel it. Cut into thin slices and set aside.

Wash the mint thoroughly under cold running water and slightly drain. Torn with hands and set aside.

Now, combine carrot, mango, orange, and mint in a juicer and process until juiced. Transfer to a serving glass and stir in the coconut water and honey.

Add some ice and serve immediately.

Enjoy!

Nutrition information per serving: Kcal: 217, Protein: 3.8g, Carbs: 46.6g, Fats: 1.1g

19. Cucumber Lime Juice

Ingredients:

1 cup cucumber, sliced

1 whole lime, peeled

1 cup fresh coriander, chopped

2 whole leeks, chopped

1 cup turnip greens, chopped

1 cup sweet potatoes, cubed

1 cup spinach, chopped

Preparation:

Wash the cucumber and cut into thin slices. Fill the measuring cup and reserve the rest for later. Set aside.

Peel the lime and cut lengthwise in half. Set aside.

In a large colander, combine coriander, turnip greens, and spinach. Wash thoroughly under cold running water. Chop all into small pieces and set aside.

Wash the leeks and cut into bite-sized pieces. Set aside.

Peel the sweet potato and cut into small cubes. Fill the

measuring cup and reserve the rest for later. Set aside.

Now, combine cucumber, lime, coriander, turnip greens, spinach, leeks, and sweet potatoes in a juicer. Process until well juiced.

Transfer to a serving glass and serve immediately.

Nutrition information per serving: Kcal: 264, Protein: 2.2g, Carbs: 72.8g, Fats: 13.9g

20. Orange Lime Juice

Ingredients:

1 large orange, wedged

1 whole lime, peeled

1 cup papaya, peeled

1 cup fresh mint, torn

2 oz coconut water

1 tbsp liquid honey

Preparation:

Peel the orange and divide into wedges. Cut each wedge in half and set aside.

Peel the lime and cut lengthwise in half. Set aside.

Peel the papaya and cut in half. Scoop out the seeds and cut into small chunks. Set aside.

Wash the mint thoroughly under cold running water and slightly drain. Torn with hands and set aside.

Now, combine orange, lime, papaya and mint in a juicer and process until well juiced. Transfer to a serving glass and stir in the coconut water.

Add some ice and serve immediately.

Enjoy!

Nutrition information per serving: Kcal: 200, Protein: 3.6g, Carbs: 44.7g, Fats: 0.9g

21. Beet Watercress Juice

Ingredients:

1 whole beet, sliced

1 cup watercress, torn

1 cup pomegranate seeds

1 cup watermelon, cubed

2 oz water

Preparation:

Wash and peel the beet. Remove the green parts and cut into small pieces. Set aside.

Wash the watercress thoroughly under cold running water and slightly drain. Torn with hands and set aside.

Cut the top of the pomegranate fruit using a sharp paring knife. Slice down to each of the white membranes inside of the fruit. Pop the seeds into a measuring cup and set aside.

Cut the watermelon lengthwise in half. For one cup, you'll need about one large wedge. Cut and peel the wedge. Cut into bite-sized cubes and remove the seeds. Fill the measuring cup and set aside.

Now, combine, beets, watercress, pomegranate, and watermelon in a juicer and process until well juiced.

Transfer to a serving glass and serve immediately.

Nutrition information per serving: Kcal: 131, Protein: 4.5g, Carbs: 36.1g, Fats: 1.4g

22. Cantaloupe Ginger Juice

Ingredients:

1 medium-sized cantaloupe slice

1 small ginger knob, peeled

1 large orange, peeled

1 cup cucumber, sliced

1 tbsp coconut water

Preparation:

Cut the cantaloupe in half. Scoop out the seeds and cut the wedge. Peel it and cut into small pieces. Set aside.

Peel the ginger knob and cut in small pieces. Set aside.

Peel the orange and divide into wedges. Cut each wedge in half and set aside.

Wash the cucumber and cut into thin slices. Fill the measuring cup and reserve the rest for later. Set aside.

Now, combine cantaloupe, ginger, orange, and cucumber in a juicer and process until juiced. Transfer to a serving glass and stir in the coconut water.

Refrigerate for 10-15 minutes before serving.

Nutrition information per serving: Kcal: 103, Protein: 2.7g, Carbs: 30.2g, Fats: 0.5g

23. Cantaloupe Plum Juice

Ingredients:

1 cup cantaloupe, chunked

2 large plums, pitted

1 whole kiwi, peeled

1 cup red leaf lettuce, shredded

1 tbsp liquid honey

Preparation:

Cut the cantaloupe in half. Scoop out the seeds and flesh. Cut two wedges and peel them. Chop into chunks and set aside. Reserve the rest of the cantaloupe in a refrigerator.

Wash the plums and cut in half. Remove the pits and cut into bite-sized pieces. Set aside.

Peel the kiwi and cut lengthwise in half. Set aside.

Wash the lettuce thoroughly and shred it. Fill the measuring cup and reserve the rest for later.

Now, combine kiwi, cantaloupe, plums, and lettuce in a juicer and process until juiced. Transfer to a serving glass and stir in the honey.

Add some ice and serve immediately.

Nutrition information per serving: Kcal: 136, Protein: 3.4g, Carbs: 38.6g, Fats: 1.1g

24. Ginger Pineapple Juice

Ingredients:

¼ tsp ginger, ground

1 cup pineapple, chunked

1 medium-sized carrot, sliced

1 cup cherries, pitted

1 tbsp coconut water

Preparation:

Using a sharp paring knife, cut the top of the pineapple. Gently remove all hard skin and slice it into thin slices. Fill the measuring cup and reserve the rest for later.

Wash and peel the carrot. Cut into thin slices and set aside.

Wash the cherries and cut each in half. Remove the pits and fill the measuring cup. Reserve the rest in the refrigerator.

Now, combine pineapple, carrot, and cherries in a juicer and process until well juiced. Transfer to a serving glass and stir in the ginger and coconut water. Garnish with some fresh mint and serve immediately.

Nutrition information per serving: Kcal: 175, Protein: 3.1g, Carbs: 52.1g, Fats: 0.6g

25. Grapefruit Strawberry Juice

Ingredients:

1 whole grapefruit, wedged

1 cup strawberries, chopped

1 medium-sized banana, sliced

1 small Granny Smith's apple, cored

1 tbsp coconut water

Preparation:

Peel the banana and cut into thin slices. Set aside.

Peel the grapefruit and divide into wedges. Cut each wedge in half and set aside.

Wash the strawberries and remove the stems. Cut into bite-sized pieces and fill the measuring cup. Reserve the rest for later.

Wash the apple and cut lengthwise in half. Remove the core and cut into bite-sized pieces. Set aside.

Now, combine banana, grapefruit, strawberries, and apple in a juicer and process until well juiced. Transfer to a serving glass and stir in the coconut water.

Add few ice cubes and serve immediately.

Nutrition information per serving: Kcal: 268, Protein: 4.4g, Carbs: 79.6g, Fats: 1.2g

26. Blackberry Orange Juice

Ingredients:

1 cup blackberries

1 medium-sized orange, peeled

1 cup watermelon, cubed

1 tbsp liquid honey

¼ tsp cinnamon, ground

Preparation:

Wash the blackberries thoroughly under cold water and slightly drain. Set aside.

Peel the orange and divide into wedges. Cut each wedge in half and set aside.

Cut the watermelon in half. Cut one large wedge and wrap the rest in a plastic foil and refrigerate. Peel the slice and cut into small cubes. Remove the pits and fill the measuring cup. Set aside.

Now, combine blackberries, orange, and watermelon in a juicer and process until juiced. Transfer to a serving glass and stir in the honey and cinnamon.

Refrigerate for 15 minutes before serving.

Enjoy!

Nutrition information per serving: Kcal: 186, Protein: 4.2g, Carbs: 40.7g, Fats: 1.1g

27. Cherry Banana Juice

Ingredients:

1 cup cherries, pitted

1 medium-sized banana, sliced

1 whole grapefruit, peeled

1 cup fresh mint, torn

2 tbsp coconut water

Preparation:

Wash the cherries and remove the stems, if any. Cut each cherry in half and remove the pits. Fill the measuring cup and set aside.

Peel the banana and cut into thin slices. Set aside.

Peel the grapefruit and divide into wedges. Cut each wedge in half and set aside.

Wash the mint thoroughly under cold running water and slightly drain. Torn with hands and set aside.

Now, combine cherries, banana, grapefruit, and mint in a juicer and process until juiced. Transfer to a serving glass and stir in the coconut water.

Add some crushed ice and serve immediately.

Nutrition information per serving: Kcal: 274, Protein: 5.8g, Carbs: 81.5g, Fats: 1.3g

28. Cantaloupe Lemon Juice

Ingredients:

1 small cantaloupe wedge

1 whole lemon, peeled

1 cup cherries, pitted

1 cup pineapple chunks

1 oz water

Preparation:

Cut the cantaloupe in half. Scrape out the seeds and cut one thin slice. Wrap the rest in a plastic foil and refrigerate for later.

Peel the lemon and cut lengthwise in half. Set aside.

Wash the cherries and remove the green stems, if any. Cut each cherry in half and fill the measuring cup. Set aside.

Using a sharp paring knife, cut the top of the pineapple. Gently remove all hard skin and slice it into thin slices. Fill the measuring cup and reserve the rest for later.

Now, combine cantaloupe, lemon, cherries, and pineapple in a juicer. Process until well juiced. Transfer to a serving glass and stir in the water.

Refrigerate for 10 minutes before serving. Enjoy!
Nutrition information per serving: Kcal: 176, Protein: 3.4g, Carbs: 53.6g, Fats: 0.7g

29. Carrot Peach Juice

Ingredients:

1 medium-sized honeydew melon slice

1 medium-sized carrot, sliced

1 medium-sized peach, chopped

1 small green apple, cored

Preparation:

Wash and peel the carrot. Cut into thin slices and set aside.

Wash the peach and cut in half. Remove the pit and cut small pieces. Set aside.

Cut melon lengthwise in half. Scoop out the seeds and then wash the melon. Cut one wedge and peel it. Cut into bite-sized pieces and set aside.

Wash the apple and cut in half. Remove the core and cut into bite-sized pieces. Set aside.

Now, combine carrot, peach, apple, and melon in a juicer and process until juiced. Transfer to a serving glass and refrigerate for 10-15 minutes before serving.

Nutrition information per serving: Kcal: 176, Protein: 3.2g, Carbs: 51.1g, Fats: 1g

30. Banana Apple Juice

Ingredients:

1 medium-sized banana, sliced

1 small Granny Smith's apple, cored

1 cup mango, chunked

1 cup fresh mint, torn

1 small ginger knob, peeled

1 tbsp liquid honey

Preparation:

Peel the banana and cut into thin slices. Set aside.

Wash the apple and cut in half. Remove the core and cut into bite-sized pieces. Set aside.

Peel the mango and cut into small chunks. Fill the measuring cup and reserve the rest for later. Set aside.

Place the mint in a large colander. Rinse well under cold running water and slightly drain. Torn with hands and set aside.

Peel the ginger knob and set aside.

Now, combine mango, banana, apple, mint, and ginger in a juicer and process until juiced. Transfer to a serving glass and stir in the honey.

Add few ice cubes and serve immediately.

Nutrition information per serving: Kcal: 325, Protein: 4.3g, Carbs: 76.1g, Fats: 1.6g

31. Grapefruit Avocado Juice

Ingredients:

1 whole grapefruit, peeled

1 cup avocado, cubed

1 cup beets, trimmed and sliced

½ cup green grapes

2 oz water

Preparation:

Peel the grapefruit and divide into wedges. Cut each wedge in half and set aside.

Peel the avocado and cut lengthwise in half. Cut into small cubes and fill the measuring cup. Reserve the rest for later.

Wash the beets thoroughly and trim off the green parts. Cut into thin slices and fill the measuring cup. Reserve the rest in the refrigerator.

Wash the grapes and fill the measuring cup. Set aside.

Now, combine grapefruit, avocado, beets, and grapes in a juicer. Add few ice cubes and process until juiced.

Transfer to a serving glass and stir in the water.

Serve immediately.

Nutrition information per serving: Kcal: 350, Protein: 7.3g, Carbs: 56.1g, Fats: 22.6g

32. Banana Grapefruit Juice

Ingredients:

1 cup mango, cubed

1 cup fresh mint, torn

1 large banana, sliced

1 whole grapefruit, wedged

1 oz coconut water

Preparation:

Peel the mango and cut into small cubes. Fill the measuring cup and reserve the rest for later.

Wash the mint thoroughly and torn with hands. Set aside.

Peel the banana and cut into thin slices. Set aside.

Peel the grapefruit and divide into wedges. Cut each wedge in half and set aside.

Now, combine banana, grapefruit, mango, and mint in a juicer and process until juiced. Transfer to a serving glass and stir in the coconut water. Add some ice and serve immediately.

Enjoy!

Nutrition information per serving: Kcal: 293, Protein: 5.6g, Carbs: 85.7g, Fats: 1.6g

33. Zesty Lemon Juice

Ingredients:

2 whole lemons, peeled

1 whole lime, peeled

1 large orange, wedged

1 small ginger slice, peeled

2 oz of water

Preparation:

Peel the orange and divide into wedges. Cut each wedge in half and set aside.

Peel the lemons and lime. Cut each fruit lengthwise in half and set aside.

Peel the ginger and slice into small pieces. Set aside.

Now, combine orange, lemons, lime, and ginger in a juicer and process until well juiced. Add some ice and water to the juicer and blend again for 5 seconds.

Transfer to a serving glass and garnish with some lemon slices before serving.

Enjoy!

Nutrition information per serving: Kcal: 102, Protein: 3.3g, Carbs: 36.5g, Fats: 0.6g

34. Celery Apple Juice

Ingredients:

2 medium-sized celery stalk, chopped

1 small Granny Smith's apple, cored

1 small orange, wedged

1 large strawberry, chopped

1 oz water

Preparation:

Peel the orange and divide into wedges. Set aside.

Wash the celery and cut into bite-sized pieces. Set aside.

Wash the apple and cut in half. Remove the core and cut into bite-sized pieces. Set aside.

Wash the strawberry and cut in half. Set aside.

Now, combine celery, apple, orange, and strawberry in a juicer and process until well juiced. Transfer to a serving glass and add some crushed ice.

Serve immediately.

Nutrition information per serving: Kcal: 116, Protein: 2.2g, Carbs: 34.6g, Fats: 0.6g

35. Strawberry Apple Juice

Ingredients:

1 cup fresh strawberries, chopped

1 medium-sized Granny Smith's apple, cored

1 cup pomegranate seeds

1 large carrot, sliced

Preparation:

Wash the strawberries and remove the stems. Chop into bite-sized pieces and set aside.

Wash the apple and cut in half. Remove the core and cut into bite-sized pieces. Set aside.

Cut the top of the pomegranate fruit using a sharp paring knife. Slice down to each of the white membranes inside of the fruit. Pop the seeds into a measuring cup and set aside.

Wash and peel the carrot. Cut into thin slices and set aside.

Now, combine strawberries, apple, pomegranate seeds, and carrot in a juicer and process until juiced. Transfer into a serving glass and refrigerate for 10 minutes before serving.

Enjoy!

Nutritional information per serving: Kcal: 243, Protein: 9.2g, Carbs: 32.6g, Fats: 2.3g

36. Orange Mint Juice

Ingredients:

1 small orange, peeled

1 cup fresh mint, torn

1 cup cantaloupe, diced

1 whole lemon, peeled

¼ tsp ginger, ground

Preparation:

Peel the orange and divide into wedges. Cut each wedge in half and set aside.

Wash the mint thoroughly under cold water. Slightly drain and torn with hands. Set aside.

Cut the cantaloupe in half. Scoop out the seeds and cut one medium wedge. Peel it and dice into small pieces. Reserve the rest of the cantaloupe in a refrigerator.

Peel the lemon and cut lengthwise in half. Set aside.

Now, combine orange, mint, cantaloupe, and lemon in a juicer and process until juiced. Transfer to a serving glass and stir in the ginger.

Add some ice and serve immediately.

Nutritional information per serving: Kcal: 104, Protein: 3.8g, Carbs: 33.2g, Fats: 0.8g

37. Banana Cucumber Juice

Ingredients:

1 large banana, peeled

1 cup cucumber, sliced

4 whole kiwis, peeled

2 small papaya, chopped

1 tbsp fresh mint, roughly chopped

Preparation:

Peel the banana and cut into chunks. Set aside.

Wash the cucumber and cut into thin slices. Fill the measuring cup and reserve the rest for later. Set aside.

Peel the kiwis and cut in half. Set aside.

Peel the papaya and cut in half. Remove the seeds and dice into small pieces. Set aside.

Now, combine banana, cucumber, kiwis, papaya, and mint in a juicer and process until juiced. Transfer to a serving glass and add some ice before serving.

Enjoy!

Nutritional information per serving: Kcal: 365, Protein: 6.5g, Carbs: 107g, Fats: 2.8g

38. Pear Lemon Juice

Ingredients:

1 large pear, chopped

1 whole lemon, peeled

1 cup raspberries

1 small Granny Smith's apple, cored

1 oz water

Preparation:

Wash the pear and cut in half. Remove the core and cut into bite-sized pieces. Set aside.

Peel the lemon and cut lengthwise in half. Set aside.

Wash the raspberries thoroughly using a colander. Slightly drain and set aside.

Wash the apple and cut in half. Remove the core and cut into small pieces. Set aside.

Now, combine pear, lemon, raspberries, and apple in a juicer and process until juiced. Transfer to a serving glass and stir in the water.

Add some ice before serving and enjoy!

Nutritional information per serving: Kcal: 214, Protein: 3.6g, Carbs: 74.7g, Fats: 1.6g

39. Grapefruit Lettuce Juice

Ingredients:

1 whole grapefruit, wedged

1 cup Romaine lettuce, shredded

2 medium-sized carrots, sliced

1 cup fresh mint, chopped

1 whole lime, peeled

Preparation:

Peel the grapefruit and divide into wedges. Cut each wedge in half and set aside.

Wash the lettuce thoroughly under cold running water. Shred it and fill the measuring cup. Reserve the rest for later.

Wash and peel the carrots. Cut into thin slices and set aside.

Wash the mint and then place it in a medium bowl. Add one cup of hot water and let it soak for 10 minutes. Slightly drain and set aside.

Peel the lime and cut lengthwise in half. Set aside.

Now, combine grapefruit, lettuce, carrots, mint, and lime in a juicer and process until juiced. Transfer to a serving glass and add some crushed ice before serving.

Enjoy!

Nutritional information per serving: Kcal: 147, Protein: 4.7g, Carbs: 46.8g, Fats: 1.1g

40. Lime Apricot Juice

Ingredients:

1 whole lime, peeled

1 cup apricots, sliced

2 large peaches, pitted

1 large banana, peeled

Preparation:

Peel the lime and roughly chop it. Make sure to reserve lime juice while cutting.

Wash the apricots and cut in half. Remove the pits and cut into small pieces. Fill the measuring cup and set aside.

Wash the peaches and cut in half. Remove the pits and cut each half into bite-sized pieces. Set aside.

Peel the banana and cut into small chunks. Set aside.

Now, combine lime, apricots, peaches, and banana in a juicer and process until juiced. Transfer to a serving glass and add some crushed ice before serving.

Enjoy!

Nutritional information per serving: Kcal: 299, Protein: 7.2g, Carbs: 86.5g, Fats: 2g

41. Papaya Cherry Juice

Ingredients:

1 small papaya, chopped

1 cup sour cherries, halved

1 cup avocado, cubed

1 whole lemon, peeled

¼ tsp cinnamon, ground

1 oz water

Preparation:

Peel the papaya and cut into small chunks. Set aside.

Rinse the cherries using a large colander. Cut in half and remove the pits. Fill the measuring cup and set aside.

Peel the avocado and cut lengthwise in half. Remove the pit and cut into small cubes. Fill the measuring cup and reserve the rest for later.

Peel the lemon and cut lengthwise in half. Set aside.

Now, combine papaya, cherries, avocado, and lemon in a juicer and process until juiced. Transfer to a serving glass and stir in the cinnamon and water.

Refrigerate for 10 minutes before serving and enjoy!

Nutritional information per serving: Kcal: 343, Protein: 5.8g, Carbs: 57.3g, Fats: 22.8g

42. Vanilla Pineapple Juice

Ingredients:

1 cup pineapple, chunked

1 cup green grapes

1 tsp vanilla extract

2 oz cold water

Preparation:

Cut the top of a pineapple. Using a sharp paring knife, peel it and cut into thin slices. Fill the measuring cup and reserve the rest for later.

In a heavy-bottomed pot, combine grapes and one cup of water. Bring it to a boil over a medium-high temperature, stirring occasionally. Stir in the vanilla extract and remove from the heat. Set aside to cool completely.

Now, combine grape mixture and pineapple in a juicer and process until well juiced. Transfer to a serving glass and stir in the water.

Refrigerate for about 15 minutes before serving.

Nutritional information per serving: Kcal: 200, Protein: 2.1g, Carbs: 57g, Fats: 0.8g

43. Sweet Plum Apple Juice

Ingredients:

2 whole plums, pitted

1 small Golden Delicious apple, cored

1 cup pomegranate seeds

1 large strawberry, chopped

1 tbsp liquid honey

2 oz water

Preparation:

Wash the plums and cut lengthwise in half. Remove the pits and cut into small pieces. Set aside.

Wash the apple and cut in half. Remove the core and cut into bite-sized pieces. Set aside.

Cut the top of the pomegranate fruit using a sharp paring knife. Slice down to each of the white membranes inside of the fruit. Pop the seeds into a measuring cup and set aside.

Wash the strawberry and remove the stem. Cut into small pieces and set aside.

Now, combine, plums, apple, pomegranate seeds, and

strawberry in a juicer and process until juiced. Transfer to a serving glass and add some crushed ice.

Serve immediately.

Nutritional information per serving: Kcal: 176, Protein: 2.8g, Carbs: 50.3g, Fats: 1.6g

44. Cherry Apricot Juice

Ingredients:

1 cup cherries, pitted

1 whole apricot, pitted

1 whole guava, peeled

1 medium-sized orange, wedged

Preparation:

Wash the cherries using a colander. Remove the stems and cut each in half. Remove the pits and fill the measuring cup. Set aside.

Wash the apricot and cut in half. Remove the pit and cut into bite-sized pieces. Set aside.

Peel the guava and cut into small chunks. Set aside.

Peel the orange and divide into wedges. Cut each wedge in half and set aside.

Now, combine cherries, apricot, guava, and orange in a juicer and process until juiced. Transfer to a serving glass and add some ice.

Serve immediately.

Nutritional information per serving: Kcal: 173, Protein: 4.7g, Carbs: 51.8g, Fats: 1.1g

45. Cucumber Lime Juice

Ingredients:

1 cup cucumber, sliced

1 whole lime, peeled

2 cups collard greens, chopped

1 cup Swiss chard, chopped

1 large celery stalk, chopped

1 oz water

¼ tsp salt

Preparation:

Wash the cucumber and cut into thin slices. Fill the measuring cup and reserve the rest in the refrigerator.

Peel the lime and cut lengthwise in half. Set aside.

Combine collard greens and Swiss chard in a large colander. Wash it under running water and slightly drain. Chop into small pieces and set aside.

Wash the celery and cut into small pieces. Set aside.

Now, combine cucumber, lime, collard greens, Swiss chard,

and celery in a juicer and process until juiced. Transfer to a serving glass and stir in the water and salt. Refrigerate for 10 minutes before serving.

Enjoy!

Nutritional information per serving: Kcal: 40, Protein: 3.8g, Carbs: 12.7g, Fats: 0.7g

46. Orange Coconut Juice

Ingredients:

1 small orange, pee ed

1 tbsp coconut water

2 whole apricots, pitted

2 whole plums, chopped

1 cup cherries, pitted

Preparation:

Peel the orange and divide into wedges. Cut each wedge in half and set aside.

Wash the apricots and cut in half. Remove the pits and cut all into small pieces. Set aside.

Wash the plums and cut in half. Remove the pits and cut into bite-sized pieces. Set aside.

Wash the cherries using a colander. Remove the pits and set aside.

Now, combine orange, apricots, plums, and cherries in a juicer and process until well juiced. Transfer to a serving glass and stir in the coconut water.

Refrigerate for 5 minutes before serving.

Enjoy!

Nutritional information per serving: Kcal: 191, Protein: 4.3g, Carbs: 56.3g, Fats: 1.1g

47. Blackberry Lemon Juice

Ingredients:

1 cup blackberries

1 whole lemon, peeled

1 cup pomegranate seeds

1 medium-sized carrot, sliced

1 oz water

Preparation:

Wash the blackberries using a colander. Fill the measuring cup and reserve the rest. Set aside.

Peel the lemon and cut lengthwise in half. Set aside.

Cut the top of the pomegranate fruit using a sharp paring knife. Slice down to each of the white membranes inside of the fruit. Pop the seeds into a measuring cup and set aside.

Wash and peel the carrot. Cut into thin slices and set aside.

Now, combine blackberries, lemon, pomegranate seeds, and carrot in a juicer. Process until juiced and transfer to a serving glass.

Add some ice or refrigerate for a while before serving.

Nutritional information per serving: Kcal: 119, Protein: 4.6g, Carbs: 41.3g, Fats: 2.1g

48. Banana Strawberry Juice

Ingredients:

1 large banana, chopped

1 large strawberry, chopped

3 whole kiwis, peeled

1 small apple, cored

¼ tsp cinnamon, ground

Preparation:

Peel the banana and chop into small chunks. Set aside.

Wash the strawberry and remove the stem. Cut into small pieces and set aside.

Peel the kiwis and cut lengthwise in half. Set aside.

Wash the apple and cut in half. Remove the core and cut into bite-sized pieces. Set aside.

Now, combine banana, strawberry, kiwi, and apple in a juicer and process until juiced. Transfer to a serving glass and stir in the cinnamon.

Refrigerate for 5 minutes before serving.

Enjoy!

Nutritional information per serving: Kcal: 292, Protein: 4.4g, Carbs: 85g, Fats: 1.9g

49. Raspberry Peach Juice

Ingredients:

1 cup raspberries

1 small peach, pitted

1 cup mango, chunked

3 whole apricots, chopped

1 oz water

Preparation:

Rinse the raspberries using a colander. Slightly drain and fill the measuring cup. Reserve the rest in the refrigerator or freezer for later.

Wash the peach and cut in half. Remove the pit and cut into bite-sized pieces. Set aside.

Peel the mango and cut into small chunks. Fill the measuring cup and reserve the rest for later.

Wash the apricots and cut in half. Remove the pits and cut in quarters. Set aside.

Now, combine raspberries, peach, mango, and apricots in a juicer and process until juiced. Transfer to a serving glass and stir in the water.

Refrigerate for 10 minutes before serving.

Nutritional information per serving: Kcal: 206, Protein: 5.5g, Carbs: 63.5g, Fats: 2.1g

50. Zucchini Citrus Juice

Ingredients:

1 medium-sized zucchini, sliced

1 whole lime, peeled

1 whole lemon, peeled

1 cup fresh mint, chopped

2 oz water

Preparation:

Wash the zucchini and cut into thin slices. Set aside.

Peel the lemon and lime. Cut each fruit into quarters and set aside.

Rinse the mint thoroughly under cold running water. Slightly drain and chop into small pieces. Set aside.

Now, combine basil, zucchini, lemon, and lime in a juicer. Process until well juiced. Transfer to a serving glass and stir in the water.

Refrigerate for 10 minutes before serving.

Nutritional information per serving: Kcal: 50, Protein: 3.9g, Carbs: 15.8g, Fats: 0.9g

51. Lemon Cucumber Juice

Ingredients:

1 whole lemon, peeled

1 cup cucumber, sliced

1 whole beet, sliced

1 medium-sized orange, peeled

1 tbsp liquid honey

1 oz water

Preparation:

Peel the lemon and cut into quarters. Set aside.

Wash the cucumber and cut into thin slices. Fill the measuring cup and reserve the rest in the refrigerator.

Wash the beet and trim off the green parts. Cut into thin slices and set aside.

Peel the orange and divide into wedges. Cut each wedge in half and set aside.

Now, combine lemon, cucumber, beet, and orange in a juicer and process until juiced. Transfer to a serving glass and stir in the honey and water.

Add some ice and serve immediately.

Nutritional information per serving: Kcal: 154, Protein: 3.5g, Carbs: 30.5g, Fats: 0.5g

52. Plums 'n Greens Juice

Ingredients:

4 whole plums, chopped

1 cup Romaine lettuce, shredded

1 cup mustard greens, torn

1 cup baby carrots, sliced

1 oz of water

Preparation:

Wash the plums and cut each in half. Remove the pits and set aside.

Combine lettuce and mustard greens in a large colander. Rinse well under cold running water. Shred the lettuce torn the mustard greens using hands. Set aside.

Wash and peel the carrots. Cut into thin slices and fill the measuring cup. Reserve the rest in the refrigerator.

Now, combine plums, lettuce, mustard greens, and carrots in a juicer and process until juiced. Transfer to a serving glass and stir in the water.

Enjoy!

Nutritional information per serving: Kcal: 128, Protein: 4.8g, Carbs: 39.1g, Fats: 1.3g

53. Kiwi Tea Juice

Ingredients:

2 whole kiwis, peeled

1 tsp green tea

2 tbsp hot water

1 medium-sized pear, chopped

1 cup fresh spinach, torn

1 cup fresh mint, roughly chopped

1 whole lime, peeled

Preparation:

Peel the kiwis and cut lengthwise in half. Set aside.

Combine green tea and hot water in a small bowl. Stir well and set aside to soak for 3 minutes.

Wash the pear and remove the core. Cut into bite-sized pieces and set aside.

Wash the spinach under cold running water using a colander. Torn with hands and set aside.

Wash the mint and roughly chop it. Fill the measuring cup

and reserve the rest for later.

Peel the lime and cut lengthwise in half. Set aside.

Now, combine kiwis, green tea mixture, pear, spinach, mint, and lime in a juicer and process until juiced. Transfer to a serving glass and add some ice before serving.

Enjoy!

Nutritional information per serving: Kcal: 195, Protein: 9.4g, Carbs: 62.4g, Fats: 2.1g

ADDITIONAL TITLES FROM THIS AUTHOR

70 Effective Meal Recipes to Prevent and Solve Being Overweight: Burn Fat Fast by Using Proper Dieting and Smart Nutrition

By Joe Correa CSN

48 Acne Solving Meal Recipes: The Fast and Natural Path to Fixing Your Acne Problems in Less Than 10 Days!

By Joe Correa CSN

41 Alzheimer's Preventing Meal Recipes: Reduce or Eliminate Your Alzheimer's Condition in 30 Days or Less!

By Joe Correa CSN

70 Effective Breast Cancer Meal Recipes: Prevent and Fight Breast Cancer with Smart Nutrition and Powerful Foods

By Joe Correa CSN

www.ingramcontent.com/pod-product-compliance
Lightning Source LLC
Chambersburg PA
CBHW052027070526
44584CB00016B/1936